Caribou

By Roman Patrick

 **Gareth Stevens**
Publishing

Please visit our Web site, www.garethstevens.com. For a free color catalog of all our high-quality books, call toll free 1-800-542-2595 or fax 1-877-542-2596.

Library of Congress Cataloging-in-Publication Data

Patrick, Roman.
  Caribou / Roman Patrick.
      p. cm. – (Animals that live in the tundra)
  Includes index.
  ISBN 978-1-4339-3897-9 (pbk.)
  ISBN 978-1-4339-3898-6 (6-pack)
  ISBN 978-1-4339-3896-2 (library binding)
  1. Caribou–Juvenile literature. 2. Tundra animals–Juvenile literature. I. Title.
  QL737.U55P367 2011
  599.65'8–dc22

                                    2010000403

First Edition

Published in 2011 by
Gareth Stevens Publishing
111 East 14th Street, Suite 349
New York, NY 10003

Designer: Michael J. Flynn
Editor: Therese Shea

Photo credits: Cover, p. 1, back cover John E. Marriott/All Canada Photos/
Getty Images; pp. 5, 7, 9, 11 (inset), 15 Shutterstock.com; p. 11 Tom Walker/
Photographers Choice/Getty Images; p. 13 Johnny Johnson/The Image Bank/
Getty Images; p. 17 Wayne R. Bilenduke/The Image Bank/Getty Images; p. 19
Max Dereta/Workbook Stock/Getty Images; p. 21 Oliver Morin/AFP/Getty Images.

Printed in the United States of America

CPSIA compliance information: Batch #CS10GS: For further information contact Gareth Stevens, New York, New York at 1-800-542-2595.

Table of Contents

Boldface words appear in the glossary.

All About Caribou

You may know caribou by another name—reindeer! "Caribou" is the name used for wild reindeer in **North America**. Caribou can be found in the **tundra**.

Male caribou are as tall as an adult man. They weigh a lot more, though! **Females** are a little smaller. Both grow **antlers**. Males fight each other with their antlers.

antlers

Caribou have white coats in winter. It is hard to see them in the snow. They have brown coats in summer. These coats blend in, too. Both coats keep them warm in the cold tundra.

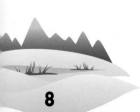

coat in winter

9

Caribou have special hoofs. They dig in the snow with their hoofs to look for food. Their hoofs keep them from falling on ice and rocks. They also help caribou swim.

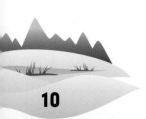

hoofs

Life on the Go

Caribou eat a lot. In summer, they eat grass and plants in the tundra. In winter, the tundra is covered with snow. Caribou go south to find food.

Caribou travel in herds. Up to 500,000 caribou travel together to forests thousands of miles away. There, they dig for food such as reindeer moss.

herd

In spring, the tundra grows plants again. Mother caribou are the first to return. Their calves grow strong eating tundra plants.

calf

Caribou Hunters

Caribou have enemies, such as bears and wolves. If a caribou spots danger, it warns other caribou. It puts its tail in the air and holds its head high. Then, it runs!

People hunt caribou. In the far north, people eat caribou meat and use their furs. Antlers are made into tools. Caribou can also pull loads. Have you ever seen a caribou pull a sled?

Fast Facts

Height	up to 5 feet (1.5 meters) at the shoulder
Length	up to 7 feet (2.1 meters)
Weight	up to 700 pounds (320 kilograms); females are smaller
Diet	grass and plants, such as reindeer moss
Average life span	about 15 years in the wild

Glossary

antler: a bony, branched growth on the head of an animal

female: a girl

male: a boy

North America: the landform made up of the United States, Canada, Greenland, and Mexico

tundra: flat, treeless plain with ground that is always frozen

For More Information

Books

Frost, Helen. *Caribou.* Mankato, MN: Capstone Press, 2007.

Heuer, Karsten. *Being Caribou: Five Months on Foot with a Caribou Herd.* New York, NY: Walker, 2007.

Quinlan, Susan E. *Caribou.* Minneapolis, MN: Carolrhoda Books, 2005.

Web Sites

National Geographic: Caribou
animals.nationalgeographic.com/animals/mammals/caribou.html
Read "fast facts" about caribou and see a video about their antlers.

National Parks: Caribou
www.eparks.org/wildlife_protection/wildlife_facts/caribou.asp
See photos of caribou in action and read about woodland caribou.

Index

About the Author

Roman Patrick is a writer of several children's books. He was born near the Arctic Circle and grew up loving the animals that lived there. He now lives in Buffalo, NY.